Surprisingly easy to crochet, six shrugs and boleros by Abbey Swanson reflect a variety of styles and yarn weights. Three are made in one size that fits most women; the others are for small, medium, and large sizes.

Ice Storm **2**
Bonfire Shrug **6**
Lilacs in May **10**
Summery Silk Shrug **14**
Azure Dream **18**
Trellis Shrug **22**
General Instructions **25**
Yarn Information **27**
Meet Abbey Swanson **28**

LEISURE ARTS, INC. • Maumelle, Arkansas

Ice Storm

EASY

SHOPPING LIST

Yarn (Light Weight) 3

[3.5 ounces, 290 yards
(100 grams, 265 meters) per skein]:

☐ 1{2-2} skein(s)

Crochet Hook

☐ Size H (5 mm)
or size needed for gauge

SIZE INFORMATION

Sizes: Small{Medium-Large}

Finished Sizes: 14" high x 35{36¾-38½}" circumference/ 35.5 cm x 89{93.5-98} cm

Size Note: We have printed the instructions for the sizes in different colors to make it easier for you to find:

- size Small in Blue
- size Medium in Pink
- size Large in Green

Instructions in Black apply to all sizes.

GAUGE INFORMATION

In pattern, one repeat (13 sts) = 2⁷/₈" (7.25 cm); 10 rows (Rows 3 and 4, 5 times) = 4½" (11.5 cm)

Gauge Swatch: 5¹/₈" wide x 2" high (13 cm x 5 cm)

Ch 24.

Work same as Wrap, page 5, for 5 rows: 22 sts and 2 chs.

Finish off.

STITCH GUIDE

FRONT POST TREBLE CROCHET ***(abbreviated FPtr)***

YO twice, insert hook from **front** to **back** around post of st indicated ***(Fig. A)***, YO and pull up a loop (4 loops on hook), (YO and draw through 2 loops on hook) 3 times.

BACK POST TREBLE CROCHET ***(abbreviated BPtr)***

YO twice, insert hook from **back** to **front** around post of st indicated ***(Fig. A)***, YO and pull up a loop (4 loops on hook), (YO and draw through 2 loops on hook) 3 times.

Fig. A

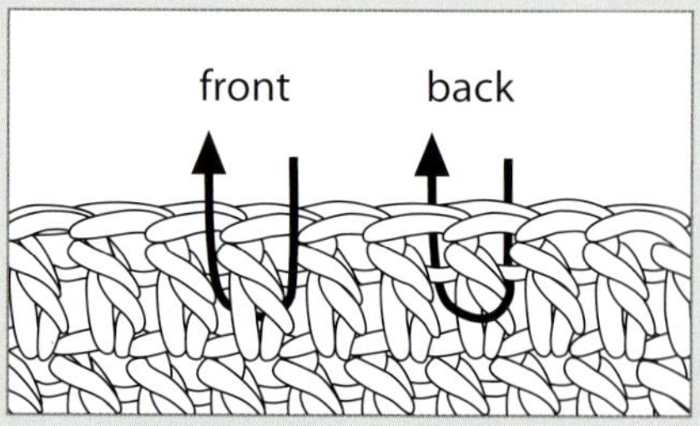

WRAP

Ch 64.

Row 1 (Right side)**:** Sc in second ch from hook and in each ch across: 63 sc.

Note: Loop a short piece of yarn around any stitch to mark Row 1 as **right** side.

Row 2: Ch 3 **(counts as first dc, now and throughout)**, turn; dc in next 4 sc, ch 1, ★ skip next sc, dc in next 12 sc, ch 1; repeat from ★ across to last 6 sc, skip next sc, dc in last 5 sc: 58 dc and 5 chs.

Row 3: Ch 3, turn; dc in next 4 dc, ch 1, skip next ch, ★ dc in next 4 dc, skip next 2 sts, work FPtr around each of next 2 sts, working in **front** of last 2 FPtr made, work FPtr around each of 2 skipped sts, dc in next 4 dc, ch 1, skip next ch; repeat from ★ across to last 5 dc, dc in last 5 dc.

Row 4: Ch 3, turn; dc in next 4 dc, ch 1, skip next ch, ★ dc in next 4 dc, work BPtr around each of next 4 FPtr, dc in next 4 dc, ch 1, skip next ch; repeat from ★ across to last 5 dc, dc in last 5 dc.

Rows 5 thru 78{82-86}: Repeat Rows 3 and 4, 37{39-41} times.

Joining Row: Ch 1, turn; with **wrong** side together, working through **both** loops of sts on last row **and** through free loops of beginning ch *(Fig. 2, page 26)*, slip st in each st across; do **not** finish off.

Top Trim

Rnd 1: Ch 1; with **right** side facing and working in end of rows, work 2 sc in each dc row around, sc in first sc row; join with slip st to first sc.

Rnd 2: Ch 1, sc in same st as joining and in each sc around; join with slip st to first sc.

Rnd 3: Slip st in each sc around; join with slip st to first slip st, finish off.

Bottom Trim

Rnd 1: With **right** side of opposite side facing and working in end of rows, join yarn with sc in first sc row *(see Joining With Sc, page 26)*; work 3 sc in each dc row around; join with slip st to first sc.

Rnd 2: Ch 1, sc in same st as joining and in each sc around; join with slip st to first sc.

Rnd 3: Slip st in each sc around; join with slip st to first slip st, finish off.

Bonfire Shrug

EASY

SHOPPING LIST

Yarn (Fine Weight)

[1.75 ounces, 163 yards
(50 grams, 150 meters) per skein]:

☐ 3{3-4} skeins

Crochet Hook

☐ Size H (5 mm)
or size needed for gauge

SIZE INFORMATION

Small{Medium-Large}

Size Note: We have printed the instructions for the sizes in different colors to make it easier for you to find:

- size Small in Blue
- size Medium in Pink
- size Large in Green

Instructions in Black apply to all sizes.

GAUGE INFORMATION

In pattern, 27 sc = 5½" (14 cm);
16 rows = 4" (10 cm)

Gauge Swatch: 5½" wide x 4" high (14 cm x 10 cm)

Work same as Body for 16 rows: 27 sc.

STITCH GUIDE

PICOT

Ch 3, slip st in top of last dc made.

SINGLE CROCHET 2 TOGETHER ***(abbreviated sc2tog)***

Pull up a loop in each of next 2 sc, YO and draw through all 3 loops on hook **(counts as one sc)**.

BODY

Ch 28.

Row 1 (Right side)**:** Sc in second ch from hook and in each ch across: 27 sc.

Note: Loop a short piece of yarn around any stitch to mark Row 1 as **right** side.

Row 2: Ch 1, turn; sc in Front Loop Only of each sc across ***(Fig. 1, page 26)***.

Row 3: Ch 1, turn; sc in Back Loop Only of each sc across.

Repeat Rows 2 and 3 for pattern until Body measures approximately 41{44-47}"/104{112-119.5} cm from beginning ch, ending by working Row 2; do **not** finish off.

Edging Rnd: Ch 1, turn; working in both loops, 2 sc in first sc, sc in next 25 sc, 3 sc in last sc, place marker in center sc of 3-sc group for Outer Border placement; work 203{219-235} sc evenly spaced across end of rows; working in free loops of beginning ch ***(Fig. 2, page 26)***, 3 sc in first ch, sc in next 25 chs, 3 sc in last ch; work 203{219-235} sc evenly spaced across end of rows; sc in same sc as first sc; join with slip st to first sc, finish off: 468{500-532} sc.

Outer Border

Rnd 1: With **right** side facing, join yarn with dc in marked sc ***(see Joining With Dc, page 26)***, remove marker; dc in next 2 sc, ★ (dc, ch 1, dc) in next sc, dc in next 3 sc; repeat from ★ across long edge ending with last dc in center sc of next 3-sc group; being careful **not** to twist piece, join with slip st to first dc: 258{278-298} dc and 51{55-59} ch-1 sps.

Rnd 2: Ch 1, sc in same st as joining and in next dc, skip next 2 dc, (3 dc, work Picot, 2 dc) in next ch-1 sp, ★ skip next 2 dc, sc in next 3 dc and in next ch-1 sp, sc in next 3 dc, skip next 2 dc, (3 dc, work Picot, 2 dc) in next ch-1 sp; repeat from ★ around to last 4 dc, skip next 2 dc, sc in last 2 dc; join with slip st to first sc, finish off.

Shoulder Assembly

Place a marker in center sc on opposite long edge; place another marker in the 29th sc **before** marked center sc.

With **wrong** side of first short end and long edge together and working through **inside** loops on **both** edges, join yarn with slip st in second marked sc **and** in center sc of first 3-sc group on short end, remove marker; slip st in each st across to center marked sc, slip st in Back Loop Only of marked sc, remove marker; with **wrong** side of second short end and long edge together and continuing to work through **inside** loops on **both** edges, slip st in each st across; do **not** finish off.

First Armhole Edging

Rnd 1 (Right side)**:** Working in remaining 73{81-89} sc around armhole edge, sc in first sc, ★ sc2tog, sc in next 7{8-9} sts; repeat from ★ around; join with slip st to first sc: 65{73-81} sc.

Rnd 2: Ch 1, sc in same st as joining and in each sc around; join with slip st to first sc.

Rnd 3: Ch 1, sc in same st as joining and in next 6{7-8} sc, sc2tog, ★ sc in next 6{7-8} sc, sc2tog; repeat from ★ around; join with slip st to first sc: 57{65-73} sc.

Rnd 4: Slip st loosely in each sc around; join with slip st to first slip st, finish off.

Second Armhole Edging

Rnd 1: With **right** side facing and working in remaining 73{81-89} sts around second armhole edge, join yarn with sc in first unworked sc after Shoulder Assembly; ★ sc2tog, sc in next 7{8-9} sts; repeat from ★ around; join with slip st to first sc: 65{73-81} sc.

Rnd 2: Ch 1, sc in same st as joining and in each sc around; join with slip st to first sc.

Rnd 3: Ch 1, sc in same st as joining and in next 6{7-8} sc, sc2tog, ★ sc in next 6{7-8} sc, sc2tog; repeat from ★ around; join with slip st to first sc: 57{65-73} sc.

Rnd 4: Slip st loosely in each sc around; join with slip st to first slip st, finish off.

Lilacs in May

EASY **Finished Size:** One size fits most

SHOPPING LIST

Yarn (Light Weight) LIGHT 3

[3.5 ounces, 306 yards
(100 grams, 280 meters) per skein]:

- ☐ Off White - 1 skein
- ☐ Lavender - 1 skein
- ☐ Berry - 1 skein
- ☐ Mauve - 1 skein

Crochet Hook

- ☐ Size H (5 mm)
  or size needed for gauge

GAUGE INFORMATION

In pattern, (3 dc, ch 1) 5 times and 9 rnds = 4" (10 cm)

Gauge Swatch:

3⁵/₈" (9.25 cm) square

Work same as Body through Rnd 4: 48 dc and 16 sps.

BODY

With Off White, ch 4; join with slip st to form a ring.

Rnd 1 (Right side)**:** Ch 5 **(counts as first dc plus ch 2, now and throughout)**, (3 dc in ring, ch 2) 3 times, 2 dc in ring; join with slip st to first dc: 12 dc and 4 ch-2 sps.

Note: Loop a short piece of yarn around any stitch to mark Rnd 1 as **right** side.

Rnd 2: (Slip st, ch 5, 2 dc) in next ch-2 sp, dc in next dc, ch 1, skip next dc, dc in next dc, ★ (2 dc, ch 2, 2 dc) in next ch-2 sp, dc in next dc, ch 1, skip next dc, dc in next dc; repeat from ★ 2 times **more**, dc in same sp as first dc; join with slip st to first dc: 24 dc and 8 sps.

Rnd 3: (Slip st, ch 5, 3 dc) in next corner ch-2 sp, ch 1, 3 dc in next ch-1 sp, ch 1, ★ (3 dc, ch 2, 3 dc) in next corner ch-2 sp, ch 1, 3 dc in next ch-1 sp, ch 1; repeat from ★ 2 times **more**, 2 dc in same sp as first dc; join with slip st to first dc: 36 dc and 12 sps.

Rnd 4: (Slip st, ch 5, 3 dc) in next corner ch-2 sp, ch 1, (3 dc in next ch-1 sp, ch 1) twice, ★ (3 dc, ch 2, 3 dc) in next corner ch-2 sp, ch 1, (3 dc in next ch-1 sp, ch 1) twice; repeat from ★ 2 times **more**, 2 dc in same sp as first dc; join with slip st to first dc, finish off: 48 dc and 16 sps.

Rnd 5: With **right** side facing, join Lavender with dc in any corner ch-2 sp ***(see Joining with Dc, page 26)***; ch 2, 3 dc in same sp, ch 1, ★ (3 dc in next ch-1 sp, ch 1) across to next corner ch-2 sp, (3 dc, ch 2, 3 dc) in corner sp, ch 1; repeat from ★ 2 times **more**, (3 dc in next ch-1 sp, ch 1) across, 2 dc in same sp as first dc; join with slip st to first dc, finish off: 60 dc and 20 sps.

Rnd 6: With **right** side facing, join Berry with dc in any corner ch-2 sp; ch 2, 3 dc in same sp, ch 1, ★ (3 dc in next ch-1 sp, ch 1) across to next corner ch-2 sp, (3 dc, ch 2, 3 dc) in corner sp, ch 1; repeat from ★ 2 times **more**, (3 dc in next ch-1 sp, ch 1) across, 2 dc in same sp as first dc; join with slip st to first dc, finish off: 72 dc and 24 sps.

Rnd 7: With **right** side facing, join Mauve with dc in any corner ch-2 sp; ch 2, 3 dc in same sp, ch 1, ★ (3 dc in next ch-1 sp, ch 1) across to next corner ch-2 sp, (3 dc, ch 2, 3 dc) in corner sp, ch 1; repeat from ★ 2 times **more**, (3 dc in next ch-1 sp, ch 1) across, 2 dc in same sp as first dc; join with slip st to first dc, finish off: 84 dc and 28 sps.

Rnd 8: With **right** side facing, join Lavender with dc in any corner ch-2 sp; ch 2, 3 dc in same sp, ch 1, ★ (3 dc in next ch-1 sp, ch 1) across to next corner ch-2 sp, (3 dc, ch 2, 3 dc) in corner sp, ch 1; repeat from ★ 2 times **more**, (3 dc in next ch-1 sp, ch 1) across, 2 dc in same sp as first dc; join with slip st to first dc, finish off: 96 dc and 32 sps.

Rnds 9-17: Repeat Rows 6-8, 3 times: 204 dc and 68 sps.

Rnd 18: With Off White, repeat Rnd 7: 216 dc and 72 sps.

Rnds 19-25: Repeat Rnd 8 once, then repeat Rnds 6-8 twice: 300 dc and 100 sps.

Rnd 26: With Off White, repeat Rnd 7: 312 dc and 104 sps.

Rnds 27-30: Repeat Rnd 8 once, then repeat Rnds 6-8 once: 360 dc and 120 dc.

Rnd 31: With **right** side facing, join Off White with dc in any corner ch-2 sp; ch 2, 3 dc in same sp, ch 1, ★ (3 dc in next ch-1 sp, ch 1) across to next corner ch-2 sp, (3 dc, ch 2, 3 dc) in corner sp, ch 1; repeat from ★ 2 times **more**, (3 dc in next ch-1 sp, ch 1) across, 2 dc in same sp as first dc; join with slip st to first dc, do **not** finish off: 372 dc and 124 sps.

Rnd 32-35: (Slip st, ch 5, 3 dc) in next corner ch-2 sp, ch 1, ★ (3 dc in next ch-1 sp, ch 1) across to next corner ch-2 sp, (3 dc, ch 2, 3 dc) in corner sp, ch 1; repeat from ★ 2 times **more**, (3 dc in next ch-1 sp, ch 1) across, 2 dc in same sp as first dc; join with slip st to first dc: 420 dc and 140 sps.

Finish off.

Rnds 36-40: Repeat Rnd 8 once, then repeat Rnds 6 and 7 twice; at end of Rnd 40, do **not** finish off: 480 dc and 160 sps.

First Side Joining: With Mauve, slip st in next corner ch-2 sp; fold piece in half with **wrong** side together and matching sts, working through **inside** loops of **both** layers, slip st in second ch of corners and in next 3 dc, (slip st in next ch and in next 3 dc) 9 times; finish off.

Second Side Joining: Working on opposite side and continuing to work through **inside** loops of **both** layers, join Mauve with slip st in second ch of corners; slip st in next 3 dc, (slip st in next ch and in next 3 dc) 9 times; finish off.

Trim

Rnd 1: With **right** side facing, join Berry with dc in either Side Joining; 2 dc in same st, ch 1, (3 dc in next ch-1 sp, ch 1) across to next Side Joining, 3 dc in joining, ch 1, (3 dc in next ch-1 sp, ch 1) across; join with slip st to first dc, finish off: 240 dc and 80 ch-1 sps.

Rnd 2: With **right** side facing, join Mauve with dc in any ch-1 sp; 2 dc in same sp, ch 1, (3 dc in next ch-1 sp, ch 1) around; join with slip st to first dc, finish off.

Rnd 3: With **right** side facing, join Lavender with dc in any ch-1 sp; 2 dc in same sp, ch 1, (3 dc in next ch-1 sp, ch 1) around; join with slip st to first dc, finish off.

Summery Silk Shrug

EASY

Finished Size: One size fits most

SHOPPING LIST

Yarn (Light Weight) LIGHT 3

[2.2 ounces, 102 yards

(65 grams, 93 meters) per ball]:

- ☐ Grey - 2 balls
- ☐ Gold - 2 balls
- ☐ Blue - 2 balls

Crochet Hook

- ☐ Size 7 (4.5 mm)

  or size needed for gauge

GAUGE INFORMATION

In pattern, 16 sts = 4" (10 cm);
12 rows = 4¾" (12 cm)

Gauge Swatch: 4½" wide x 4¾" high (11.5 cm x 12 cm)

With Grey, ch 19.

Work same as Body for 12 rows: 18 dc.

Finish off.

BODY

With Grey, ch 109.

Row 1 (Right side)**:** Sc in second ch from hook and in each ch across: 108 sc.

Note: Loop a short piece of yarn around any stitch to mark Row 1 as **right** side.

Row 2: Ch 3 **(counts as first dc, now and throughout)**, turn; dc in next sc, ch 2, ★ skip next 2 sc, dc in next sc, ch 2; repeat from ★ across to last 4 sc, skip next 2 sc, dc in last 2 sc: 38 dc and 70 chs.

Row 3: Ch 1, turn; sc in each st across changing to Gold in last sc ***(Fig. 3a, page 26)***: 108 sc.

Row 4: Ch 3, turn; dc in next sc and in each sc across changing to Blue in last dc ***(Fig. 3b, page 26)***.

Row 5: Ch 1, turn; sc in each dc across.

Row 6: Ch 3, turn; dc in next sc, ch 2, ★ skip next 2 sc, dc in next sc, ch 2; repeat from ★ across to last 4 sc, skip next 2 sc, dc in last 2 sc: 38 dc and 70 chs.

Row 7: Ch 1, turn; sc in each st across changing to Gold in last dc: 108 sc.

Row 8: Ch 3, turn; dc in next sc and in each sc across changing to Grey in last dc.

Row 9: Ch 1, turn; sc in each dc across.

Row 10: Ch 3, turn; dc in next sc, ch 2, ★ skip next 2 sc, dc in next sc, ch 2; repeat from ★ across to last 4 sc, skip next 2 sc, dc in last 2 sc: 38 dc and 70 chs.

Row 11: Ch 1, turn; sc in each st across changing to Gold in last sc: 108 sc.

Rows 12-15: Repeat Rows 4-7 changing to Grey at end of last row.

Row 16: Ch 3, turn; dc in each sc across changing to Gold in last dc.

Row 17: Ch 1, turn; sc in each dc across.

Row 18: Ch 3, turn; dc in next sc, ch 2, ★ skip next 2 sc, dc in next sc, ch 2; repeat from ★ across to last 4 sc, skip next 2 sc, dc in last 2 sc: 38 dc and 70 chs.

Row 19: Ch 1, turn; sc in each st across changing to Grey in last sc: 108 sc.

Row 20: Ch 3, turn; dc in next sc and in each sc across changing to Blue in last dc.

Row 21: Ch 1, turn; sc in each dc across.

Row 22: Ch 3, turn; dc in next sc, ch 2, ★ skip next 2 sc, dc in next sc, ch 2; repeat from ★ across to last 4 sc, skip next 2 sc, dc in last 2 sc: 38 dc and 70 chs.

Row 23: Ch 1, turn; sc in each st across changing to Grey in last dc: 108 sc.

Rows 24-27: Repeat Rows 16-19 changing to Blue at end of last row.

Row 28: Ch 3, turn; dc in next sc and in each sc across changing to Grey in last dc.

Row 29: Ch 1, turn; sc in each dc across.

Row 30: Ch 3, turn; dc in next sc, ch 2, ★ skip next 2 sc, dc in next sc, ch 2; repeat from ★ across to last 4 sc, skip next 2 sc, dc in last 2 sc: 38 dc and 70 chs.

Row 31: Ch 1, turn; sc in each st across changing to Blue in last dc: 108 sc.

Row 32: Ch 3, turn; dc in next sc and in each sc across changing to Gold in last dc.

Row 33: Ch 1, turn; sc in each dc across.

Row 34: Ch 3, turn; dc in next sc, ch 2, ★ skip next 2 sc, dc in next sc, ch 2; repeat from ★ across to last 4 sc, skip next 2 sc, dc in last 2 sc: 38 dc and 70 chs.

Row 35: Ch 1, turn; sc in each st across changing to Blue in last dc: 108 sc.

Rows 36-39: Repeat Rows 28-31 changing to Gold at end of last row.

Rows 40-63: Repeat Rows 4-27; at end of last row, finish off.

First Side Trim: With **wrong** side facing and working in end of rows, join Blue with sc in first sc on Row 1 *(see Joining With Sc, page 26)*; work 99 sc evenly spaced across; finish off: 100 sc.

Second Side Trim: With **wrong** side facing and working in end of rows on opposite side of Body, join Blue with sc in first sc on Row 63; work 99 sc evenly spaced across changing to Grey in last sc; do **not** finish off: 100 sc.

Border: Ch 1, turn; sc in each sc across to last sc, 2 sc in last sc; sc in each sc across Row 63; 2 sc in first sc on First Side Trim, sc in each sc across; finish off.

ASSEMBLY

Fold Body in half, having **wrong** side together and matching first and last rows of Body.

Joining: Working through **both** layers across short end and through **inside** loops of Border sts, join Grey with slip st in first sc; slip st in next 9 sc; do **not** finish off.

Arm Opening - Rnd 1: Continuing around single layer of Border, sc in both loops of each sc around *(Fig. 1, page 26)*; join with slip st to first sc.

Rnd 2: Ch 1, sc in same st as joining and in each sc around; join with slip st to first sc, finish off.

Repeat Joining and Arm Opening across opposite short end.

Outer Border - Rnd 1: With **right** side facing and working in free loops of beginning ch *(Fig. 2, page 26)*, join Grey with sc in first ch *(see Joining With Sc, page 26)*; sc in each ch across; sc in each sc across Border; join with slip st to first sc.

Rnd 2: Ch 1, sc in same st as joining and in each sc around; join with slip st to first sc; finish off.

Azure Dream

EASY

SHOPPING LIST

Yarn (Light Weight) LIGHT 3

[3.5 ounces, 245 yards (100 grams, 224 meters) per skein]:

- ☐ Ecru - 1{2-2} skein(s)
- ☐ Blue - 1{1-2} skein(s)

Crochet Hook

- ☐ Size 7 (4.5 mm) **or** size needed for gauge

SIZE INFORMATION

Small{Medium-Large}

Size Note: We have printed the instructions for the sizes in different colors to make it easier for you to find:

- size Small in Blue
- size Medium in Pink
- size Large in Green

Instructions in Black apply to all sizes.

GAUGE INFORMATION

17 dc = 4" (10 cm);
10 rows = 4¼" (10.75 cm)

Gauge Swatch: 4" wide x 4¼" high (10 cm x 10.75 cm)

With Ecru, ch 19.

Row 1: Dc in fourth ch from hook **(3 skipped chs count as first dc)** and in each ch across: 17 dc.

Rows 2-10: Ch 3 **(counts as first dc)**, turn; dc in next dc and in each dc across.

Finish off.

STITCH GUIDE

TREBLE CROCHET ***(abbreviated tr)***

YO twice, insert hook in sp or sp indicated, YO and pull up a loop (4 loops on hook), (YO and draw through 2 loops on hook) 3 times.

SINGLE CROCHET 2 TOGETHER ***(abbreviated sc2tog)***

Pull up a loop in each of next 2 dc, YO and draw through all 3 loops on hook **(counts as one sc)**.

DOUBLE CROCHET 2 TOGETHER ***(abbreviated dc2tog)*** (uses next 2 sts)

★ YO, insert hook in **next** st, YO and pull up a loop, YO and draw through 2 loops on hook; repeat from ★ once **more**, YO and draw through all 3 loops on hook **(counts as one dc)**.

DOUBLE DECREASE (uses next 3 sts)

YO, † insert hook in **next** st, YO and pull up a loop, YO and draw through 2 loops on hook †, YO, skip **next** st, repeat from † to † once, YO and draw through all 3 loops on hook **(counts as one dc)**.

SHRUG

With Ecru and beginning at neck edge, ch 124; place marker in third ch from hook for Neck Trim placement.

Row 1 (Right side)**:** Dc in fourth ch from hook **(3 skipped chs count as first dc)** and in next 23 chs, (dc, ch 1, dc) in next ch, dc in next 6 chs, (dc, ch 1, dc) in next ch, dc in next 56 chs, (dc, ch 1, dc) in next ch, dc in next 6 chs, (dc, ch 1, dc) in next ch, dc in last 25 chs: 126 dc and 4 ch-1 sps.

Note: Loop a short piece of yarn around any stitch to mark Row 1 as **right** side.

Row 2: Ch 3 **(counts as first dc, now and throughout)**, turn; ★ dc in next dc and in each dc across to next ch-1 sp, (dc, ch 1, dc) in ch-1 sp; repeat from ★ 3 times **more**, dc in next dc and in each dc across: 134 dc and 4 ch-1 sps.

Rows 3 thru 11{12-13}: Ch 3, turn; ★ dc in next dc and in each dc across to next ch-1 sp, (dc, ch 1, dc) in ch-1 sp; repeat from ★ 3 times **more**, dc in next dc and in each dc across: 206{214-222} dc and 4 ch-1 sps.

Row 12{13-14}: Ch 3, turn; ★ dc in next dc and in each dc across to next ch-1 sp, ch 10{11-12}, skip ch-1 sp, next 28{30-32} dc, and next ch-1 sp (for armhole opening); repeat from ★ once **more**, dc in next dc and in each dc across: 150{154-158} dc and 20{22-24} chs.

Row 13{14-15}: Ch 3, turn; dc in next dc and in each dc and each ch across: 170{176-182} dc.

Row 14{15-16}: Ch 3, turn; dc in next dc and in each dc across to last dc increasing 1{0-0} dc ***(see Zeros, page 26)***, dc in last dc changing to Blue ***(Fig. 3b, page 26)***; cut Ecru: 171{176-182} dc.

Bottom Trim

Row 1: Ch 6 (**counts as first dc plus ch 3, now and throughout**), turn; ★ skip next 4 dc, (dc, ch 2, dc) in next dc, ch 3; repeat from ★ across to last 5{5-6} dc, skip next 4{4-5} dc, dc in last dc: 68{70-72} dc and 67{69-71} sps.

Row 2: Ch 4 (**counts as first tr, now and throughout**), turn; skip next ch-3 sp, (5 tr in next ch-2 sp, skip next ch-3 sp) across to last dc, tr in last dc: 167{172-177} tr.

Row 3: Ch 6, turn; skip next 2 tr, (dc, ch 2, dc) in next tr, ch 3, ★ skip next 4 tr, (dc, ch 2, dc) in next tr, ch 3; repeat from ★ across to last 3 tr, skip next 2 tr, dc in last tr: 68{70-72} dc and 67{69-71} sps.

Row 4: Ch 4, turn; skip next ch-3 sp, (5 tr in next ch-2 sp, skip next ch-3 sp) across to last dc, tr in last dc; finish off: 167{172-177} tr.

Neck Trim

Row 1: With **wrong** side facing and working in free loops of beginning ch ***(Fig. 2, page 26)***, join Blue with dc in marked ch ***(see Joining With Dc, page 26)***, remove marker; dc2tog, dc in next 21 chs, double decrease, dc in next 4 chs, double decrease, dc in next 54 chs, double decrease, dc in next 4 chs, double decrease, dc in next 21 chs, dc2tog, dc in last ch: 112 dc.

Row 2: Ch 3, turn; dc2tog, dc in next 19 dc, double decrease, dc in next 2 dc, double decrease, dc in next 52 dc, double decrease, dc in next 2 dc, double decrease, dc in next 19 dc, dc2tog, dc in last dc; finish off: 102 dc.

Edging

With **right** side facing and working in tr on Row 4 of Bottom Trim, join Blue with sc in first tr ***(see Joining With Sc, page 26)***; sc in same st and in next 2 tr, 3 sc in next tr, (sc in next 4 tr, 3 sc in next tr) across to last 3 tr, sc in next 2 tr, 3 sc in last tr; working in end of rows, 3 sc in first row, 2 sc in next row, 3 sc in next row, 2 sc in each of next 9{10-11} rows, † sc in next row, ch 31, slip st in second ch from hook and in each ch across (tie), sc in end of same row as last sc †, 2 sc in each of next 7 rows; working in dc across Row 2 of Neck Trim, 3 sc in first dc, sc in next 20 dc, sc2tog twice, sc in next 52 dc, sc2tog twice, sc in next 20 dc, 3 sc in last dc; working in end of rows, 2 sc in each of first 7 rows, repeat from † to † once, 2 sc in each of next 9{10-11} rows, 3 sc in next row, 2 sc in next row, 3 sc in next row, sc in same tr as first sc; join with slip st to first sc, finish off.

Armhole Edging

With **right** side facing and working in free loops of chs at underarm, join Blue with sc in first ch; sc in each ch across, 2 sc in side of next dc, sc in next ch-1 sp, sc in each unworked dc across to next ch-1 sp, sc in ch-1 sp, 2 sc in side of next dc; join with slip st to first sc, finish off.

Repeat around second armhole.

Trellis Shrug

EASY **Finished Size:** One size fits most

SHOPPING LIST

Yarn (Bulky Weight)

BULKY 5

[3.5 ounces, 148 yards
(100 grams, 136 meters) per skein**]**:

☐ 2 skeins

Crochet Hook

☐ Size J (6 mm) **or** size needed for gauge

GAUGE INFORMATION

In pattern,
(sc, ch 4) 4 times = 4" (10 cm);
6 rows = 3½" (9 cm)

Gauge Swatch: 5¼" wide x 3½" (13.25 cm x 9 cm)

Ch 22.

Work same as Body for 6 rows: 5 sps.

Finish off.

BODY

Ch 62.

Row 1 (Right side)**:** Sc in sixth ch from hook, ★ ch 5, skip next 3 chs, sc in next ch; repeat from ★ across: 15 ch-5 sps.

Note: Loop a short piece of yarn around any stitch to mark Row 1 as **right** side.

Rows 2-38: Ch 5, turn; sc in next ch-5 sp, (ch 5, sc in next ch-5 sp) across.

First End

Rows 1-3: Ch 5, turn; sc in next ch-5 sp, (ch 5, sc in next ch-5 sp) across to last ch-5 sp, leave last ch-5 sp unworked: 12 ch-5 sps.

Joining: Ch 3; fold Body in half lengthwise with **wrong** side together, sc in first ch-5 sp of Row 3; matching loops at end of rows and working through **both** loops as if they were one, (ch 3, sc in next loop) twice; finish off.

Second End

Row 1: With **right** side facing and working in free loops and sps across beginning ch ***(Fig. 2, page 26)***, join yarn with sc in first ch ***(see Joining With Sc, page 26)***; (ch 5, sc in next ch-3 sp) across to last ch-5 sp, leave last ch-5 sp unworked: 14 ch-5 sps.

Rows 2 and 3: Ch 5, turn; sc in next ch-5 sp, (ch 5, sc in next ch-5 sp) across to last ch-5 sp, leave last ch-5 sp unworked: 12 ch-5 sps.

Joining: Ch 3; fold Body in half lengthwise with **wrong** side together, sc in first ch-5 sp of Row 3; matching loops at end of rows and working through **both** loops as if they were one, (ch 3, sc in next loop) twice; finish off.

General Instructions

ABBREVIATIONS

BPtr	Back Post treble crochet(s)
ch(s)	chain(s)
cm	centimeters
dc	double crochet(s)
dc2tog	double crochet 2 together
FPtr	Front Post treble crochet(s)
mm	millimeters
Rnd(s)	Round(s)
sc	single crochet(s)
sc2tog	single crochet 2 together
sp(s)	space(s)
st(s)	stitch(es)
tr	treble crochet(s)
YO	yarn over

CROCHET TERMINOLOGY		
UNITED STATES		INTERNATIONAL
slip stitch (slip st)	=	single crochet (sc)
single crochet (sc)	=	double crochet (dc)
half double crochet (hdc)	=	half treble crochet (htr)
double crochet (dc)	=	treble crochet (tr)
treble crochet (tr)	=	double treble crochet (dtr)
double treble crochet (dtr)	=	triple treble crochet (ttr)
triple treble crochet (tr tr)	=	quadruple treble crochet (qtr)
skip	=	miss

SYMBOLS & TERMS

★ — work instructions following ★ as many **more** times as indicated in addition to the first time.

† to † — work all instructions from first † to second † **as many** times as specified.

( ) or **[ ]** — work enclosed instructions **as many** times as specified by the number immediately following **or** work all enclosed instructions in the stitch or space indicated **or** contains explanatory remarks.

colon (:) — the number(s) given after a colon at the end of a row or round denote(s) the number of stitches or spaces you should have on that row or round.

GAUGE

Exact gauge is **essential** for proper size/fit. Before beginning your project, make the sample swatch given in the individual instructions in the yarn and hook specified. After completing the swatch, measure it, counting your stitches and rows/rounds carefully. If your swatch is larger or smaller than specified, **make another, changing hook size to get the correct gauge**. Keep trying until you find the size hook that will give you the specified gauge.

CROCHET HOOKS																	
U.S.	B-1	C-2	D-3	E-4	F-5	G-6	7	H-8	I-9	J-10	K-10½	L-11	M/N-13	N/P-15	P/Q	Q	S
Metric - mm	2.25	2.75	3.25	3.5	3.75	4	4.5	5	5.5	6	6.5	8	9	10	15	16	19

BEGINNER	Projects for first-time crocheters using basic stitches. Minimal shaping.
EASY	Projects using yarn with basic stitches, repetitive stitch patterns, simple color changes, and simple shaping and finishing.
INTERMEDIATE	Projects using a variety of techniques, such as basic lace patterns or color patterns, mid-level shaping and finishing.
EXPERIENCED	Projects with intricate stitch patterns, techniques and dimension, such as non-repeating patterns, multi-color techniques, fine threads, small hooks, detailed shaping and refined finishing.

JOINING WITH SC

When instructed to join with a sc, begin with a slip knot on hook. Insert hook in stitch or space indicated, YO and pull up a loop, YO and draw through both loops on hook.

JOINING WITH DC

When instructed to join with a dc, begin with a slip knot on hook. YO, holding loop on hook, insert hook in stitch or space indicated, YO and pull up a loop (3 loops on hook), (YO and draw through 2 loops on hook) twice.

ZEROS

To consolidate the length of an involved pattern, zeros are sometimes used so that all sizes can be combined. For example, dc in next dc and in each dc across to last dc increasing 1{0-0} dc means the first size would increase 1 dc and the second and last sizes would not increase at all.

BACK OR FRONT LOOPS ONLY

Work only in loop(s) indicated by arrow ***(Fig. 1)***.

Fig. 1

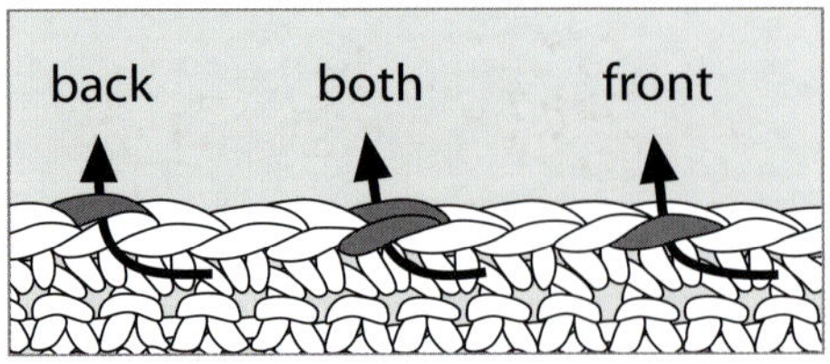

FREE LOOPS OF A CHAIN

When instructed to work in free loops of a chain, work in loop indicated by arrow ***(Fig. 2)***.

Fig. 2

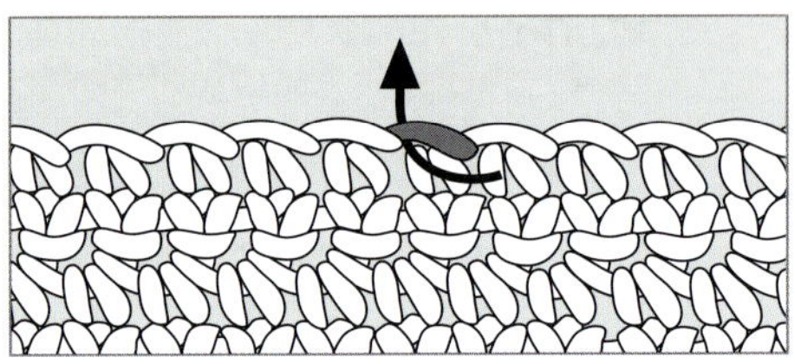

CHANGING COLORS

Work the last stitch to within one step of completion, hook new yarn ***(Fig. 3a or Fig. 3b)*** and draw through both loops on hook

Fig. 3a

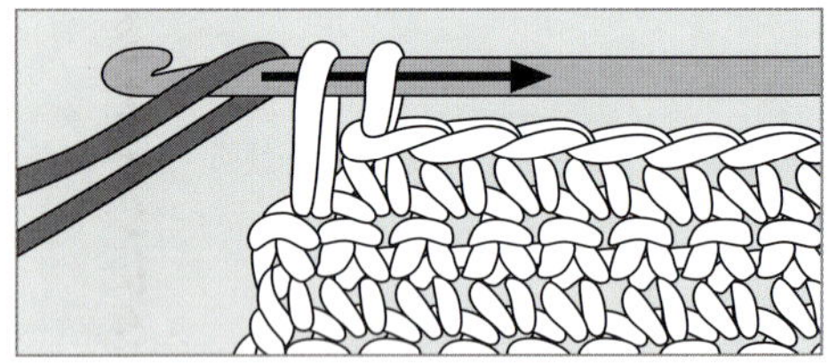

Fig. 3b

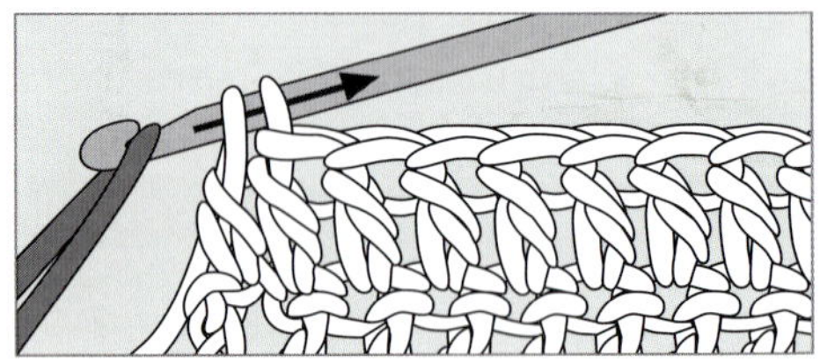

Yarn Weight Symbol & Names	LACE 0	SUPER FINE 1	FINE 2	LIGHT 3	MEDIUM 4	BULKY 5	SUPER BULKY 6	JUMBO 7
Type of Yarns in Category	Fingering, size 10 crochet thread	Sock, Fingering, Baby	Sport, Baby	DK, Light Worsted	Worsted, Afghan, Aran	Chunky, Craft, Rug	Super Bulky, Roving	Jumbo, Roving
Crochet Gauge* Ranges in Single Crochet to 4" (10 cm)	32-42 sts**	21-32 sts	16-20 sts	12-17 sts	11-14 sts	8-11 sts	6-9 sts	5 sts and fewer
Advised Hook Size Range	Steel*** 6 to 8, Regular hook B-1	B-1 to E-4	E-4 to 7	7 to I-9	I-9 to K-10½	K-10½ to M/N-13	M/N-13 to Q	Q and larger

*GUIDELINES ONLY: The chart above reflects the most commonly used gauges and hook sizes for specific yarn categories.

** Lace weight yarns are usually crocheted with larger hooks to create lacy openwork patterns. Accordingly, a gauge range is difficult to determine. Always follow the gauge stated in your pattern.

*** Steel crochet hooks are sized differently from regular hooks–the higher the number, the smaller the hook, which is the reverse of regular hook sizing.

Yarn Information

The items in this book were made using a variety of yarn weights. Any brand of the specified weight of yarn may be used. It is best to refer to the yardage/meters when determining how many balls or skeins to purchase. Remember, in order for your item to be the correct size, it is not the brand of yarn that matters, but the GAUGE/TENSION that is important.

For your convenience, listed below are the yarns used to create our photography models. Because yarn manufacturers made frequent changes in their product lines, you may sometimes find it necessary to use a substitute yarn or to search for the discontinued product at alternate suppliers (locally or online).

ICE STORM
Mary Maxim® Prism
#2013 Seascape

BONFIRE SHRUG
LB Collection® Silk
#202 Pegasus

LILACS IN MAY
LB Collection® Superwash Merino
Off White - #098 Antique
Lavender - #146 Wisteria
Berry - #141 Wild Berry
Mauve - #145 Eggplant

SUMMERY SILK SHRUG
Patons® Silk Bamboo™
Grey - #85046 Stone
Gold - #85607 Saffron
Blue - #85219 Sea

AZURE DREAM
LB Collection® Cotton Bamboo
Ecru - #098 Magnolia
Blue - #107 Hyacinth

TRELLIS SHRUG
Patons® Shetland Chunky™
#78008 Aran

Meet Abbey Swanson

A designer and artist, Abbey Swanson is passionate about crochet that is functional, wearable, and gorgeous.

"I am inspired by the beauty found both in nature and in architecture and love seeing how specific elements and color schemes translate to a pattern," she says. Abbey discovered her love for designing crochet after she made an owl hat for her son and then began designing hats for craft fairs.

"I love making items that are elegant yet simple to create," she says. Teaching crochet classes has helped her become attuned to what makes sense to crocheters at various skill levels. "I think this is a major reason my designs aren't overly complicated."

Abbey says her mission is to motivate a new generation of crocheters with designs that move beyond the granny square into a new and fresh reputation for crochet. More about Abbey and her business, The Firefly Hook, may be found at thefireflyhook.wordpress.com or on Etsy, Ravelry, Craftsy, and Facebook.

Abbey and her husband live with their three "wildly energetic and creative children" in a bustling lake town near Minneapolis, Minnesota. "My husband and I enjoy exploring with them on nature walks and fostering a love of learning in our home."

Production Team: Instructional/Technical Editor - Linda A. Daley; Editorial Writer - Susan Frantz Wiles; Senior Graphic Artist - Lora Puls; Graphic Artist - Kellie McAnulty; Photo Stylist - Lori Wenger; and Photographer - Jason Masters.

Made In U.S.A.